Other Gift books in the series
To the most, most special Sister
To the most, most special Dad
To the most, most special Grandma
Wishing you Happy Days
Thinking of You...

Published in 2014 by Helen Exley® in Great Britain.

Dedicated to Kezia, the most lovely of granddaughters.

The illustrations by Juliette Clarke and the design,
selection and arrangement © Helen Exley Creative Ltd 2014.
Words by Pam Brown © Helen Exley Creative Ltd 2014.
The moral right of the author has been asserted.

ISBN: 978-1-84634-836-5

12 11 10 9 8 7 6 5 4

Helen Exley®
16 Chalk Hill, Watford, Herts.
WD19 4BG, UK.
www.helenexley.com

You can follow us on [f] and [Y]

To the Most, most special Granddaughter

ILLUSTRATIONS BY JULIETTE CLARKE
WORDS BY PAM BROWN

HELEN EXLEY®

Light!
Spring
Joy!

Granddaughters are just the people
to take a walk with
on a bright spring day.
They match the weather.

A granddaughter
lends her grandparents
something of her joy.

A granddaughter
flings a window open
– letting in light and the
scent of Spring.

A granddaughter brings new life.
A new and lovely greening spring
from winter branches.
A promise of blossom.
A promise of rich harvest.
A new beginning.

So new

How lucky I am
to have been at your beginning..
and watch you grow.
An astonishment every day.

New granddaughters
are like special little plants,
straight from the nursery –
neat and pretty and
bursting with life.
But granddaughters grow.
And grow. And grow.
And in the end produce
the most astonishing
and incredible blooms.
That's the excitement
of granddaughters.

New Life

Just when life had settled
there came delight!
There came a new beginning.
Here came love.

A new life.
A thing most beautiful.
Something of myself
given to the future
and yet a link
with all that's gone before.
But bringing hope
to all that is to come.

A granddaughter
brings hope.

Granddaughters fill empty arms.
Bring new excitements,
new delights.
Re-awaken heart and mind.

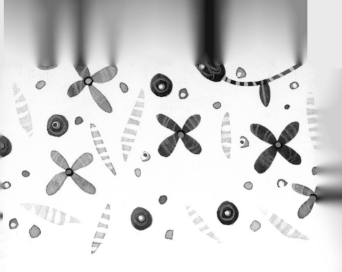

Bonus o

You are the bonus in my life –
the unexpected, the undeserved.
I watch you grow.
I watch you discover the world.
I watch you become wise
and gentle. You are a treasure.

Most kind. Most dear.
Most lovely. My granddaughter.

When all the other loves have grown old,
a new love comes to see one
through the winter years. A grandchild.

A new life
for me

Youth comes again,
enthusiasm and delight.
Curiosity. Discovery.
A joy in life.
And grandmas rouse
from non-existence
and learn to laugh again.

A granddaughter is a bonus –
to astound and delight.
I am ten years younger because of you.

Where are you going?
Somewhere exciting.
Somewhere I've never been.
Watching you I re-discover joy,
hope, wonder.
You lift my heart
as nothing else can do.

I feel young again!

Being a grandma allows you
to do it all again. Swings and slides
and roller coasters. Liquorice sticks
and chocolate cookies.
Mud and sand and flying kites.
Thank you my lovely lass
for all you've given me.

When I show you something
you have not seen before, I see it as if,
for me too, it is a new experience.

"Look, Grandma, look.
What's that? How old? How tall?
How ever did they do it? Smell this rose,
Grandma. Listen to that bird!"
The world opens like a flower.
I've come alive.

Life to you!

Here are gifts for you.
Gulls scything the summer air.
Cats drowsing in sunlight. Snow.
Laughter and song and friendship.
My gifts for you. The gift of life.

I hug myself to think of all that awaits yo
Mountains and forests,
lakes and oceans, a million creatures
to astound and delight you.
And a treasure house of things that thos
who have gone before
have fashioned for you.
Books and poems, monuments
and paintings, music of every sort.
How rich you are.

I have not much to leave you –
but one small jewel.
Shining.
Green and white and blue
and beautiful beyond belief.
Infinitely precious.
Irreplaceable.
I leave it in your care.
The planet Earth.

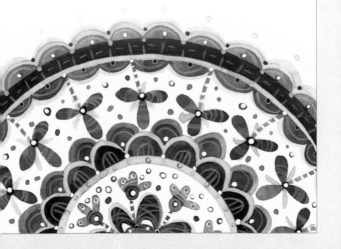

CHAOS

Grandchildren can undo,
wriggle through, squash under
and climb over any barrier in their path.
That is why most grandparents
have white hair.

Granddaughters are made of
sugar and spice and all things nice.
And mud
and peppermint and glue
and melted chocolate...

The door opens and one is lost in
a scrummage of arms and upturned faces.
Hands take your hand and you are dragged,
a happy captive, to see the wonders
treasured-up for you – the new kitten,
a dish of snail shells, a cactus in full flower,
a painting, a model cat, a tooth...

A granddaughter leaves a little ruin
and a lot of love behind her.

Naughty us!

Grandparents and grandchildren
Get Up To Things.

Every child needs a grown-up
fellow conspirator.
That's what grandparents are made for.

Grandmas and granddaughters
have a special bond.
They are both scallywags at heart
and watch each other's backs.
Covering each other's tracks.
Getting each other out of scrapes.
Comforting each other
when they're caught.
A conspiracy of two.

Caring
for me

I value above all else
the concern you've shown for me...
Love beyond your years.
And when the world seems black,
I remember.

My granddaughter is
all that I once was.
Sharp of ear and eye.
Straight of back.
Strong of heart and wind.
I toddle after her
– delighting in her youth.
And, bless her heart,
she stops and waits for me.

Granddaughters keep one young
by refusing to recognise that one is old.
"Give us a hand with these
lengths of piping, Grandma."
"Take the other end of the sofa. Lift."
"I'll dig. You sieve."
"Just give the car a shove."
"Hurry up, Grandma,
or we'll miss the bus."

A grandparent's gifts

Grandmas spend their time
looking for little things
to delight and amaze their
granddaughters.

Grandmas give granddaughters
the pretty things
they couldn't have themselves.

Grandparents have time to listen,
time to tell you stories
and time to go down to the bottom
of the garden
and see what you have discovered.

The world seems very wide
and very demanding.
Don't be afraid.
Take it a step at a time.

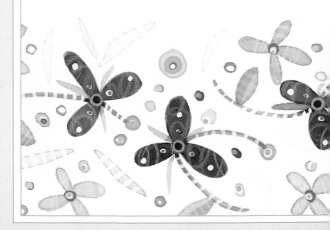

t!

Go where I have never been.
See the things I've never seen.
Be braver,
wiser than I ever was.

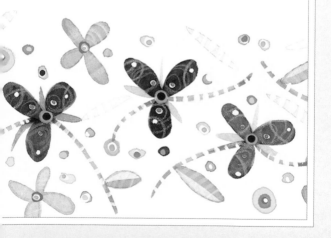

Your gifts
to me

You have given me so much.
Cuddles and kisses.
Stone-cold cups of tea.
Plasticine pots.
Loving letters. Time.

Thank you for pebbles and dandelions,
earthworms and earwigs,
fluff-covered toffees, drawings of houses,
clay polar bears, letters and kisses.

A grandma treasures
the bottle of Devon violets
as if it were the perfumes
of Arabia.
Because it's bottled love.

Grandmas have a box full
of every letter,
every card you've written.
Drawings. Cut outs.
Fairground trophies.
Snippets of your life.
Treasures.

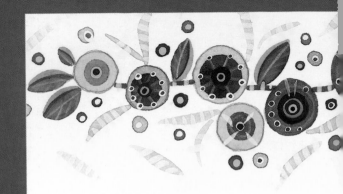

Putting

Never forget, I'm on your side –
whatever you want to be –
an airline pilot
or a ship's captain or a dentist
or a vet or a bus driver or a lady in a store
Just as long as it's worth doing –
and you put into it
everything you've got.

verything in...

More than anything,
I hope you will never be
one of those who,
looking back,
sigh and say
"I could have done great things
if I had only tried."

You!

Not a moment of your childhood
is ever lost
– I hold it in my heart.

One needs a granddaughter
to ooh and aah and hug you in delight.

A grandchild
is the cherry on the cake.

Grandmas treasure little things
a curl of hair, a splendid splodge of paint,
a crooked pot, a letter. A photograph.
A phone call. A smile. A hug.

The love gift for you!

Of course grandmothers
would love to give their granddaughters
splendid gifts. Beautiful clothes,
magical toys, adventures, books
and pictures, ponies and puppies
and kittens and cockatoos.
They do what they can –
but all they can really promise
is their love.
Forever.

Granddaughters fall off,
over and through things.
Granddaughters get stuck in,
up and under things. Granddaughters
can open anything. Granddaughters
have a homing instinct on mud.
Granddaughters scent the presence
of water, and head for it
like thirsty buffalo.
Granddaughters scream loudly.

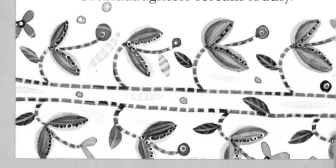

However. Granddaughters give
you handfuls of squashed raspberries.
Granddaughters give you their very best
earthworm. And frog. And caterpillar.
Granddaughters write you letters.
Granddaughters call you to tell you
they've learned their nine times table.
And then recite it. Granddaughters give you
fluff-covered toffees.
Granddaughters give you sticky kisses.

We tw

Two noses against the glass
of the display case.
A grandparent and a grandchild
making discoveries together.

Grandmas and granddads
are built to fit exactly any grandchildren
who curl up on their knees.

ogether

Here we are,
two generations touching.
To you, my childhood is unbelievable.
To me, your future is a mystery.
Two puzzles, yet both of us are on
the same road. Companions.

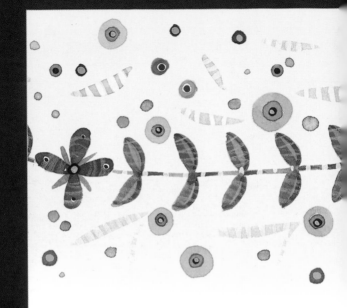

Rediscoverir
life itself

For you the world is new-minted.
And "Come and see! Come and see!"
is an instruction to me
to rediscover long lost marvels.

A grandchild under eight
is invariably sticky.
– But what's a touch of
sticky between friends?

A sticky, mes

ind of love

A granddaughter can exhaust you,
aggravate you, eat you out of house
and home – but then she clambers bonily
on to your knee, clasps buttery fingers
around your neck, plants
raspberry-tasting kisses on your face
and says, "I do love it here!"
And who cares if there's mud
and wet leaves clear through
the entire house?

If I could...

Of course I wish you
the gifts of kindness and patience
and understanding –
but peppered with curiosity,
courage, imagination, experimentation,
a capacity to doubt and, when necessary,
a streak of stubbornness.

The best I can wish you
is good companions on your journey,
enough achieved to satisfy your heart,
if not your pocket, quiet sleep
and a spattering of golden days
to cheer the heart.

How I wish I could wave
a glittery wand
and make the world safe for you.
But it was never safe –
and never will be.
Instead, I wish you courage,
intelligence and a hopeful heart.
And a little bit of luck.

Poor
Grandma!

Grandmothers love to be asked to do
up their granddaughters' shoelaces.
The trouble is, their tummies get in the way,
or their knees lock.
Grandmothers love to be asked
to watch their granddaughters
play in hockey matches. The trouble is,
they shout for the wrong side.
Grandmothers love to be asked
to their granddaughter's school play.
The trouble is they doze off halfway
through, or applaud too loudly.

Granddaughters must remember
that their grandmothers' hearts
are very willing
– but our flesh is past its best.

Granddaughters watch one
fiddling for a bit
– then take the device away from you.
"Look, Grandma. It's simple."

BRINGING U

Grandchildren are a little worried
by the presence of grandmothers
at their play. They have a word
with them, but still suspect
they may applaud too loudly.

GRANDPARENTS

Granddaughters press knobs,
stab keys,
peer knowingly at screens.
Bless them, they will explain.
Given half a chance.
Sad that they might as well
be talking Mandarin.

Laughs!

Very, very small granddaughters
memorise your phone number.
They don't speak.
They just get you out of the bath!

Her teacher asked
my very small granddaughter
to plan the house of her dreams.
She had her priorities.
A loo.
A shower.
A big armchair.
A gas stove
and a swimming pool.
A clown.
A giraffe.
And a poorly elephant.
I especially liked the elephant.

Granddaughters don't see anything
silly in a small, fat grandmother
demonstrating entrechats and pliés.

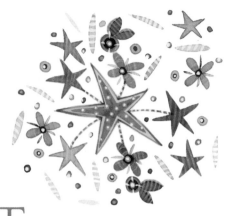

Thank you for all the joys that you have given me. The first sight of your little perfect hands.

Your first glad smile of recognition.

Your first tip-tilting steps into the safety of my arms. All the wise and funny things you had to say.

All the dazzling, unexpected gifts.

All the secrets shared. All the triumphs, big and small.

Thank you
for it all

All the muddles brought for me to unravel.
Tales of adventure, of journeys,
friendships and astonishments.
Accounts of troubles overcome,
of lessons learned.
Marvels of discovery – and love.
Courage in disappointment and in loss.
Laughter.
It was worth waiting for –
this overlapping of our lives.

Granddaughters teach you how
to do finger paintings and model clay.
Granddaughters teach you poems.
And how to box.
Granddaughters teach you
how to climb trees.
And how to examine beetles
without hurting them.
Granddaughters show you how to bat,
swim, dive, ride a bike, mount
a pony, shin up ropes and hop.

Lessons for
each other

I believe that every child in the world
needs grandparents – to tell them stories
of the days before they were born,
to teach them the old skills. To listen.
To give them time.
And that is what I will always try to give you.

Grandmas can teach
their granddaughters things that the world
seems to have forgotten.

I wish you
a growing
wisdom

I wish you courage
to face pain and loss –
and wisdom to learn from them.

Time and patience are the best
gifts I feel I can give you.
And knowledge of your roots.

No architect builds
on an uncertain foundation...
Find yourself first.
Learn to recognise and use your own
abilities. Earn respect. Gather together
skills and expert knowledge.

Wishes for you

I wish you the gift of wonder
and the strength to follow where it leads.

I wish you so much – but most of all
I wish you a face that brightens
when you come into a room,
hands that reach out in welcome,
arms that will hold you close in times
of joy and times of desolation.
I wish you love.

May you have friends with whom
you can share your greatest joys.
People to whom you can turn and smile
and know they understand.